WALL STREET BULL

Bruce Lansky

𝍐Meadowbrook
Distributed by Simon and Schuster
New York

Library of Congress Cataloging-in-Publication Data

Lansky, Bruce
Wall Street bull / by Bruce Lansky
p. cm.
ISBN 0-88166-100-7 ISBN 0-671-64739-3 (Simon &
Schuster)
1. Investments — Dictionaries — Anecdotes, facetiae,
satire, etc.
2. Finance — Dictionaries — Anecdotes, facetiae, satire,
etc.
I. Title.
HG4513.L29 1987
332.6'0207 — dc19

87-16467
CIP

Published by Meadowbrook, Inc., 18318 Minnetonka
Boulevard, Deephaven, MN 55391.

BOOK TRADE DISTRIBUTION, a division of Simon &
Schuster, Inc., 1230 Avenue of the Americas, New York, NY
10020.

S&S Ordering#: 0-671-64739-3

10 9 8 7 6 5 4 3 2
Printed in the United States of America

Editor: Patricia McKernon
Copy Editor: Barbara Bergstrom
Illustrator: Bob Flaten
Interior Design: Marcie St. Clair
Cover Design: Nancy MacLean
Production Manager: Nanci J. Stoddard

Acknowledgments

I want to thank the following people for their creative contributions to *Wall Street Bull:* Betsy Buckley (Dain Bosworth, Inc.), Anthony Carideo (*Minneapolis Star and Tribune*), Laurie Holasek (PaineWebber, Inc.), and Jim McCartney (*St. Paul Pioneer Press Dispatch*).

I am also grateful to the following people for their helpful comments in reviewing the manuscript: Lee Felicetta (Dean Witter Reynolds, Inc.), Peter Jackson (Dain Bosworth, Inc.) Martin E.W. Luther, and David Runkle (Federal Reserve Bank of Minneapolis).

I also want to thank John Downes and Jordan Elliot Goodman, authors of Barron's *Dictionary of Finance and Investment Terms,* a book that was extremely helpful to me in nailing down what many of the esoteric and obscure investment terms *really* mean.

Some of the definitions in *Wall Street Bull* appeared previously in *Not Heard on the Street* by Maurice Joy, and have been reprinted with permission of its publisher, Probus Publishing.

Introduction

Say your broker's on the line. He has a hot tip about a special situation based on some inside information. So you tell the twelve staffers meeting in your office to take a break, and you pump your broker for more information.

Seems he's gotten wind of a merger fight that pits a white knight against a raider on a stock that's currently selling below book value. The securities analyst is high on the stock for fundamental reasons; the technical analyst claims it's just broken out of its accumulation area on volume, and the sky's the limit.

Want to take a flier?

Whether you're an investor or a market professional, you play out this kind of scenario every day of the week. Sometimes you win. Sometimes you lose. But the game of wits that pits you against the market is exhilarating. And you need all the help you can get just to survive. Because Wall Street really is a jungle, and nothing is exactly as it seems.

Take your stockbroker. He belongs to a fraternity of latter-day alchemists who turn customers' hard-earned money into commissions. How about the securities analyst? His job is to recommend stocks at the precise moment they reach their yearly highs. And the technical analyst? He's Wall Street's equivalent of an astrologer.

Now what do you think of your broker's hot tip?

The bottom line is — the main thing that separates the Wall Street pros from everyone else is their ability to sling Wall Street bull. When you master this fine art, you too can make six figures a year at a nine-to-three job with your feet on your desk and a telephone in your ear.

I'm not saying that you'll wake up one day to find that you've made a fortune in the financial markets just because you've read this book. No. I'm saying something a lot more important. You'll be able to succeed beyond your wildest dreams in boardrooms, bankrooms, barrooms — even bedrooms — when you learn to sling Wall Street bull like the pros.

Bruce Lansky
June 1, 1987

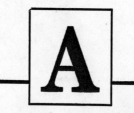

accelerated depreciation An accountant's way of recognizing what something is really worth.

accountant **1.** A professional who works with financial numbers who has too much pizazz to be an economist. **2.** The person who records management's mistakes.

account executive A financial magician who turns your hard-earned money into commissions.

accounting policy A strategy designed to make earnings look good regardless of what's really going on.

accumulation area A technical analyst's explanation of where your stock is when it isn't moving.

active market When your broker can afford to go out for lunch, but doesn't have the time.

advance/decline index According to technical analysts, if more issues advance than decline, it's bullish; if more issues decline than advance, it's bearish. What will they come up with next?

advance refunding A sophisticated technique for perpetuating the national debt.

advisory service The financial equivalent of letting Ann Landers pick your stocks.

aging schedule An accounting technique used to predict how old you'll be when a company's questionable receivables are finally collected.

air pocket stock A stock that takes you for a bumpy ride.

alligator spread How to lose your Izod in the options market.

America The land of opportunity — especially if you're a Japanese businessman.

American Depository Receipt A way to lose money on foreign stocks without leaving the country.

amortization A schedule that's too fast if you're paying back a loan and too slow if you're writing off expenses.

annual report A slick fiction that minimizes last year's fiascos by forecasting rosy days ahead.

antitrust laws What used to stop big companies from buying up their competition.

appreciation What you never get enough of from your kids or your investments.

arbitrage Buying and selling the same assets at different prices to insure the broker a profit and the investor a loss.

arrearage What preferred stockholders fall on when their dividends are omitted.

Asian CD Chinese junk.

ask price The price at which no one will buy your stock.

assets What management sits on.

at the market Abbreviation for the phrase "at the mercy of the market."

auditor's report How outsiders find out exactly how much a company's accountants lied.

authorized shares All the shares you're supposed to know about.

average This year's performance of last year's hot mutual fund.

back office The only department in a brokerage firm not ecstatic on high volume days.

bad debt The loan you made to your nephew before he left for Vegas, and some of the junk bonds in your portfolio.

balanced fund A mutual fund that strives for broad-based mediocrity.

balance of trade An economic measure that proves Americans like Japanese electronics a lot more than the Japanese like Coca-Cola.

balance sheet A document that asserts that assets equal liabilities plus investors' equity, even when the assets aren't worth anything.

balloon payment A debt obligation about to pop.

banker 1. As Mark Twain once said, "A fellow who lends you his umbrella when the sun is shining and wants it back the minute it begins to rain." **2.** A pawnbroker in a pinstriped suit.

banker's year The opposite of a baker's dozen. (There are only 360 interest-paying days on a bank's calendar.)

bankruptcy 1. When the bottom drops out of the bottom line. **2.** When it's safe to conclude that Plan A didn't work. **3.** When it's time to get back to the drawing board but the drawing board's been repossessed.

bank trust department A fast way to make a small fortune out of a large one.

bar chart 1. A graph used in annual reports to convey the opposite impression of what really transpired. **2.** A map that shows where brokers drink after the market closes.

basis point A scorekeeping system for bond traders that adds drama to an otherwise dull occupation by making gains and losses seem larger than they really are.

bear Chicken Little on Wall Street.

bear market A grizzly experience, unless you're short.

best efforts A legal responsibility that brokers take seriously only when trying to unload overpriced new issues.

beta An analytical term used by money managers to quantify the frequency, intensity, and duration of nightmares produced by a stock's volatility.

bid The price at which no one will sell you stock.

Big Board The world's most prestigious gambling casino.

Black Monday The day the lights almost went out on Wall Street.

Black Thursday Why investors TGIF.

block sale What pays the rent on Wall Street.

blue chip A stock whose reputation exceeds its performance.

blue sky laws Regulations designed to protect investors from flying in a plane in which the pilot is a crook.

board room Where the high-level office parties are held.

boiler room The place from which the broker with the get-rich-quick investment is calling.

bonds What tie up your portfolio.

book value The least your stock would be worth if a corporate raider were chasing after it.

bottom fisher An investor casting for bargains who reels in lots of sunken galoshes.

bottom line Where the red ink goes.

breakeven An optimistic investment objective.

breakout A prison term used to lend excitement to a five-point rally in the Dow.

bridge loan Money borrowed to erect a flimsy structure over a murderous ravine.

broad market Like Las Vegas: a lot of action, but not many winners.

broker An ironic title for a securities salesman because it is more descriptive of the customer.

brokerage commission Like zero and double zero on a roulette wheel, a fee that stacks the odds in favor of the house and against the investor.

bucket shop A basketball term for a sleazy brokerage firm that slam-dunks investors.

bull Pollyanna on Wall Street.

bull market When all the stocks go up except yours.

business cycle Proof that those who don't study history are doomed to repeat it.

businessman's risk An investment that's too wild for widows and orphans, and too tame for the get-rich-quick crowd.

butterfly spread A sophisticated maneuver that can leave you chloroformed and tacked to the wall in the options market.

buy and hold An investment strategy used exclusively during bear markets.

buy stop order A way to pick up a stock at its very highest price.

C

call feature A device that allows your best performing bond to be taken from you.

call option What you sell just before the stock price goes up.

call protection Something that exists only in the mind of the naive investor.

Capital Asset Pricing Model (CAPM) A sophisticated economic theory that explains, after the fact, why your investments never perform as well as you expected.

capital gains What you need to balance your capital losses.

capital in excess of par An obscure accounting term that shows how much you overpaid for your stock.

capitalization The total amount of securities issued by a corporation in an attempt to bring as many suckers into the deal as possible.

cash equivalents Various kinds of paper you receive in exchange for good hard cash.

cash flow Reported net income of a company, plus all bookkeeping deductions not paid out in actual dollars and cents; often not enough to pay all the bills.

certificate of deposit A way to lock up your money for its own protection.

charting The triumph of form over substance.

checking the market Calling your broker before ordering your drink: Chivas, bar scotch, or rotgut neat.

churning 1. What your broker does with your account on a slow day. **2.** How your broker finances his winter vacations. **3.** What your stomach does when you review your annual commission expenses.

client update When your broker tells you the good news is that the bad news could be worse.

closed-end investment company A fund whose value is often below its net asset value (a reflection of its management's reputation in the investment community).

collateral Assets pledged to secure a loan, to wit: 'Tis far better to pledge your securities to buy a house than to pledge your house to buy securities.

commercial bank A depository institution that gives you a free toaster when you bring in your bread.

commercial paper 1. Short-term parking for your cash. **2.** Cheap stuff used in gas station bathrooms.

commingled funds A way money managers disguise how badly things are going for any one account.

commissions What pay the rent on Wall Street.

commodities market A way to invest in wheat and end up with chaff.

common stock A dull name for a risky investment.

compounding What your money would be doing if you had left it in your savings account.

confidence index A reliable technical indicator based on the theory that whatever odd lot short sellers do is wrong.

conglomerate A geological term to describe a company whose management team resembles Fred Flintstone and Barney Rubble.

consolidated statement A way financial directors disguise how badly things are going for any one subsidiary.

consumer price index (CPI) An economic indicator with a rate of growth many mutual funds can't achieve.

contrarian A believer in the philosophy that fifty million Frenchmen can't be right.

conversion price The price at which you undergo a stunning religious experience.

convertible bond A bond with no top or seat belt.

Council of Economic Advisors (CEA) A group of economists whose fiscal policies aren't widely enough known to discredit.

coupon bond A bond that requires you to work for your money.

covenant A religious term describing sins a company vows never to commit in conjunction with its loan agreements.

cover What you run for when your shorts rise.

covered call writing A hedge against capital gains.

crash What happens to your net worth when the market goes into a Free-Fall.

credit analysis What you assumed your advisor did before recommending those WPPS bonds.

crown jewels Precious corporate assets that white knights will plunder after driving off corporate raiders.

cumulative preferred A provision designed to protect preferred stockholders, which ought to make you suspicious right from the start.

curb A stock exchange where it is wise to look both ways before investing.

current assets Your car, house, furniture, appliances, clothes, food, and recreational drugs.

current liabilities Your broker, your banker, your financial advisor, and your in-laws.

D

dealer A broker who trades for his own account . . . like the dealer in a card game, when no one cuts the deck.

debenture An unsecured bond, which is a lot like a loan to your son-in-law.

debt Past tense of "die."

deep discount bond What a bond becomes after you buy it.

default risk 1. The sand upon which all bonds are built. **2.** What you face if you live in California.

deficit The federal government's attempt to make you feel better about paying your VISA bill with your MasterCard.

deflation What happens after you've carefully arranged your affairs to cope with inflation.

depletion allowance A tax break that makes drilling for oil more profitable than drilling for cavities.

depreciation allowance A tax break that makes putting your house up for rent more profitable than living in it.

depression What you often feel after reading the daily stock quotations.

dilution Stock on the rocks instead of straight up.

director A sheik who hides behind the corporate veil.

direct placement Debt so attractive only the big boys get it.

disclosure What eventually happens to all useless information.

discount broker Proof that you get what you pay for.

discount rate A way for banks to make money even when they change the prime rate.

diversification Putting your eggs in too many baskets.

dividend reinvestment plan A convenient mechanism for keeping all your eggs in one basket.

dividends Payments designed to help shareholders defray the cost of their investment advisory services while waiting for their stocks to double.

---

dogs Stocks that bite the hand that feeds them.

dollar cost averaging A formula investing plan that spreads your losses over several fiscal years.

Dow Jones Industrial Average (DJIA) An index of dowdy old stocks that outperform your portfolio of growth stocks.

downtick How your broker describes a major drop in the Dow.

downturn The direction stocks take after the insiders have bailed out.

Dow theory A superstition that has survived a great deal of study and analysis.

dual purpose fund A way to divide up losses between income and capital gains.

duration The length of time your spouse carps about your investments.

early withdrawal An age-old method of family planning that fixed-term investment holders can be penalized for using.

earnings A misnomer. "Earnings and/or losses" would be more accurate.

earnings per share The same misnomer on a per-share basis.

economic forecasts Predictions inaccurate enough to make weathermen look good.

economist A professional who works with financial numbers but doesn't have the pizazz to be an accountant.

efficient market hypothesis A sophisticated theory which suggests that when someone makes money in the market he's either lucky or cheating.

end of year tax planning Locking the barn door after the horse has run away.

energy stocks Companies that get tax breaks for depleting our natural resources.

entrepreneur 1. According to authors Fisk and Barron, "A high-rolling risk-taker who would rather be a spectacular failure than a dismal success." **2.** Someone who has been in business many times.

equity Your shareholder's ownership interest in a company, if any, after deducting the debit balance in your margin account.

escrow A bank account where your money is held hostage.

estate The hovel your heirs will live in after paying inheritance taxes.

Eurobonds An investment that enables you to personally perpetuate the Marshall Plan.

ex-dividend date When you can afford to send your ex-spouse the alimony check.

execution What your broker does with your trades and you'd like to do to your broker.

extraordinary item A dignified accounting term for a wild financial transaction.

extraordinary loss A euphemism for the latest debacle.

face value Proof that you can't judge a bond by what's printed on it.

factoring An emergency cash transfusion that costs an arm and a leg.

family of funds A group of mutual funds managed by the same company. You could switch from one to another with no penalty, if only you knew when.

Fannie Mae A distant relative of Fanny Hill.

federal funds rate A borrowing rate so good it's reserved for bankers.

Federal Reserve Board (FRB) A group of economists appointed by the President to keep politics out of the economy.

fidelity bond A debt instrument whose most outstanding feature is the discrepancy between its name and its performance.

fiduciary A relationship of trust that is violated whenever the trustees think they can get away with it.

fill or kill A conditional order to buy or sell a particular security — if it isn't executed, the broker will be.

finance According to economist Robert Heilbroner, "The art of passing currency from hand to hand until it finally disappears."

Financial Accounting Standards Board (FASB) A prestigious group that understands little about accounting and less about standards.

financial adviser An affluent professional who believes that to err is human, but to be paid for it is divine.

financial risk What your investments share with the passengers on the Titanic.

first in, first out A method of accounting for inventory that also describes how insiders make money in the stock market.

fixed charges A more apt description would be "stuck" charges because no matter which way interest rates move, someone will get stuck.

flat How a bond is traded when it blows a tire.

floating rate debt A nautical term used to emphasize the constant peril of drowning in the debt market.

floor A theoretical "support" level whose holding power can only be determined *after* you've bought a stock.

foreign exchange Gresham's law in an international setting.

forward contract A way to lock up a commodity's exchange loss.

fourth market A high-stakes poker game in which the broker is dealt out.

Freddie Mac Two shares of McDonald's sandwiched around one bad mortgage, with no mustard.

free lunch What you should try to get from your broker before he's lost all your money.

free market A contradiction in terms.

full disclosure A legal requirement more honored in the breach than in the observance.

---

full-service broker A stockbroker who charges you fully for all services, whether you use them or not.

fully valued How a broker describes a stock in your portfolio he wants you to unload.

fundamental research Analysis of all the facts about a company and its industry that would enable you to make an intelligent buy/sell decision, with one exception: timing.

funded debt Long-term trouble.

fungible An attribute that listed securities share with mushrooms.

futures market A quick way to make a fortune — if the Force is with you.

generally accepted accounting principles (GAAP) A set of professional guidelines that allows the accountants to cook the books any way management wants.

general obligation bonds Debt instruments backed by the full force of a municipality's police and fire departments.

Ginnie Mae Something you would buy only after a three-martini lunch.

gnomes The Swiss banking equivalent of leprechauns.

go-go fund A mutual fund that bares its assets.

gold bug An investor who believes the worst about everything except the price of gold.

golden parachute How high-flying exec-
utives survive and prosper when their companies get hijacked.

good delivery Something you get only
from F.T.D.

goodwill The only asset left on the balance sheet of many a bankrupt company.

government bonds The safest investments on the market, except when government spending exceeds government income.

greenmail What Wall Street thugs get for mugging a weak company.

Gross National Product (GNP) An unflattering description of the economy from a macro point of view.

gross profit 1. A contradiction in terms. **2.** Preferable to a pretty loss.

growth stock A stock whose price may halve even if its earnings double.

guaranteed income contract (GIC) An attractive investment that pays out like alimony.

head and shoulders top A shampoo used just before a stock takes a bath.

hedging An action that neutralizes what would otherwise have been a profitable position.

hemline theory Low hemlines are bearish; high hemlines are bullish; pantsuits are just plain ish.

high flier According to Greek mythology, what Icarus was before the sun melted his wings.

high grade bonds A designation that "extremely safe" bonds share with frankfurters loaded with artificial colorings, flavorings, and preservatives.

high tech A stock with unlimited growth potential and a large institutional following, but little chance of showing a profit in the foreseeable future.

historical cost A meaningless cost for which accountants keep careful records.

holding company A company that owns controlling interest in one or more companies and whose major functions include: "holding" the shares, lunching with the directors, receiving and reading annual reports, attending annual meetings, voting, and complaining about their subsidiaries' products or services.

home run A baseball term for a large gain made in a short time by an investor who runs a substantial risk of striking out.

in-and-out trader A broker's ideal long-term account.

income bond A misleading name for a bond that pays interest only on those rare occasions when the company earns it.

income fund A mutual fund that provides mediocre income in return for little or no appreciation.

income statement A euphemism for a profit and loss statement.

indenture The terms under which you are bound to a bond.

index fund A fund for people who know they can't beat the market and would be happy just to match it.

individual retirement account (IRA) A
way to lose your money without sending it
to Northern Ireland.

inflation A government welfare program
to aid debtors.

in for a dime, in for a dollar What your broker says when his latest recommendation doesn't pan out.

inside information What everyone on Wall Street is looking for but may get indicted for using.

insiders Knowledgeable investors who buy before good news and sell before bad news, and later are barred from trading.

insider trading A present pastime of future cellmates.

institutional investors Lemmings.

intangible assets All those things your company has that aren't worth anything.

interest rate A percentage that's low if you're on the receiving end but high if you're on the paying end.

interest rate risk The possibility that the last payment you received was, indeed, your last.

international diversification A way to lose money in more than one country without suffering jet lag.

in the money An options term that does not necessarily describe your performance in the options market.

intrinsic value A poor substitute for market value.

investing A prudent way to make money with your money . . . for someone else.

investment banker A fancy term for a corporate fund raiser who makes more in a week than the average American family earns in a year.

investment newsletter A publication whose recommendations are often outperformed by the S&P 500, but which, nonetheless, is extremely valuable — to its publisher.

investment philosophy What your broker stresses when your portfolio is outperformed by your child's piggy bank.

investment strategy What every investor should have before rolling the dice.

investor A euphemism for someone who's locked into a big loss.

investor relations department Professionals whose job is to inform the financial community and whose hobby is to speculate in the stock market using inside information.

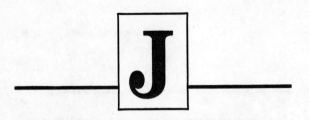

junk bonds How bargain-hunting investors finance takeovers.

justified price What the price of stocks would be if all buyers and sellers were equally naive.

Keogh plan A government-approved way to sock away tax losses for retirement.

killer bees Pinstriped assassins whose mission is to sting corporate raiders.

know your customer An ethical concept in the securities industry often satisfied by a two-martini lunch.

Laffer curve Proof that economics is neither a dismal science nor any kind of science whatsoever.

leading indicators Economic smoke signals whose meaning depends a great deal on which way the wind is blowing at the time.

lease obligations Liabilities so scary that management hides them in the footnotes of the annual report.

lender of last resort How your children view you.

lending institution A company that profits by renting money to businesses and individuals who don't need it.

letter stock Securities you couldn't get any money for even if you were allowed to sell them.

leverage A get-rich-quick scheme that often produces the opposite effect.

leveraged buyout A popular method for acquiring a company that could collapse at any moment under the weight of its debt.

liar As Bernard Baruch used to say, "anyone who claims to buy at the bottom and sell at the top."

lien What you do before you fall.

limited partnership A group of insecure investors who would rather lose money together than alone.

limit order What keeps you from buying stock before the price goes through the roof, or selling stock before the price crashes through the floor.

liquid asset The money that drains out when your portfolio springs a leak.

liquidation What happens when a company goes down for the third time.

load fund A mutual fund that can take years to earn back the up-front fee you paid when you bought it.

loan What only those who don't need can qualify for.

locked in A phrase used at cocktail parties to lead the listener to believe you've made so much off your stock you couldn't pay the taxes if you sold.

long Your position and face when the market goes down.

long range corporate plan Managementese for the directors' decision on where they'll hold the next annual meeting.

long-term debt A sophisticated way to say, "Buy now, pay much later."

long-term investment From your broker's perspective, any investment held for more than one day.

loophole The legal basis for many tax shelters.

macroeconomics The science of misreading the economy on a grand scale.

management What they try to teach in business school but actually teach better in the Army.

manipulation An overt, rampant practice prior to creation of the SEC, which has been reduced to a covert, rampant one.

margin More rope than you really need but not as much rope as you want.

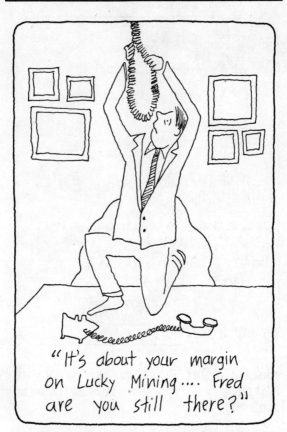

"It's about your margin on Lucky Mining.... Fred are you still there?"

margin call What you receive when all the rope you were given was too much.

market meltdown Yet another alliterative term for a seismic slump or a catastrophic crash.

market order What you may wish you had placed with your grocer instead of your broker.

market risk The possibility that you are in the right stock at the wrong time, or the wrong stock at the right time.

market slump A broker's posture when the market falls out of bed.

market value What your assets could be sold for today if you needed a tax loss.

maturity What many bonds will never see.

merger Proof that one plus one doesn't necessarily equal two.

microeconomics An excellent source of theories to explain your stock market misfortunes.

minority freeze-out A management tactic which proves the maxim that might makes right.

mixed market How your broker describes the day's trading action when some stocks go up but yours go down.

modern portfolio theory An up-to-date way to lose your shirt in the market.

monetarist A free-market economist who wants tight government control over the money supply.

monetary policy A term that dignifies the Fed's confusion and incompetence.

monetizing the debt What happens when your spouse goes shopping with your checkbook.

money manager A highly trained professional who is often outperformed by darts thrown at the *Wall Street Journal.*

money market fund An institution that yields an average rate of return for an above average risk.

money markets Where money is traded by professionals who all believe they've come away with the short end of the stick.

money supply What investors continually offer the market.

Moody's bond ratings Numbers that can produce heart attacks when lowered and deathbed cures when raised.

moral obligation bond The financial equivalent of the tooth fairy.

mortgage bond A debt instrument "secured" by a mortgage on a property that may or may not equal the value of the bonds issued against it.

municipal bond Proof that you can't fight City Hall and you shouldn't invest in it either.

mutual fund A way to get professional assistance in picking mediocre investments.

N

naked option A way to lose more than your shirt in the call market.

National Association of Securities Dealers Automated Quotation system (NASDAQ) An automated information network for O.T.C. securities that provides bid and asked quotations at which no trades can actually be executed.

national debt Pick the highest number you can think of and double it.

negotiable CD A savings vehicle you can dump without penalty when you hear a hot tip.

net asset value The true value of a load fund share, which is anywhere from 3 to 8 percent less than what you paid for it.

net profit What's left in gross profit after all real and imaginary costs have been deducted.

new issues Sure winners that your broker can't get for you, or sure losers that he can.

no load fund A type of mutual fund with a hefty management fee instead of a hefty front end fee.

nominal interest rate An apt description for the interest paid by high grade bonds.

noncallable A feature of many bonds which indicates that once you own it, management doesn't want it back again.

nonrecurring An appropriate adjective that describes the earnings of many of the companies whose shares you own.

no par An indication that accountants think a stock may be worthless.

not rated A bond so bad that Moody's refuses to look at it.

obscene profits What you often hear about but never experience yourself.

odd lot 1. What the small fry buy. **2.** Everyone connected with the securities industry.

odd lot commission A higher brokerage commission rate that persuades small investors to keep their money in banks, in mutual funds, and under mattresses.

off balance sheet financing Proof that what you can't see can hurt you.

offshore Where you go to launder money and come back with a tan.

open-end investment company A fund without a fixed capitalization that can sell shares to as many gullible investors as it can find.

open interest A rough indication of how many crazies are in the futures market.

operating lease Financial sleight-of-hand that enables a company to rent cars from a group of surgeons.

option A sophisticated technique for parlaying a small investment into a large bankroll in which your downside is limited to your entire initial investment.

option premium Proof that time is money.

original issue discount bond A bond that loses face for the underwriter when it is issued below its face value.

out of the money A horse racing term applied with equal justification to the options market.

overbought How your broker describes a stock that has advanced a few points to convince you to sell it.

overnight position A long-term commitment by day traders.

oversold How your broker describes a stock that has slipped a few points to convince you to buy it back.

oversubscribed How your broker describes the hottest new issue to explain why you can't buy any.

over the counter market (OTC) The financial version of a greasy spoon restaurant where prices are cheap and you always end up with heartburn.

panic A time-honored investment strategy whose football equivalent is the punt.

paper losses A euphemism that minimizes the impact of a decline in the value of your portfolio.

paper profits What you have plenty of until it's time to sell.

par value What stocks and bonds are theoretically (but almost never actually) worth.

payout ratio A polite way of quantifying how stingy a company is about sharing its profits with stockholders.

penetration A sexual term for piercing a stock's "resistance level" (on the upside) or "support level" (on the downside), often followed by a buying or selling climax.

pennant A formation on a stock's price chart that technical analysts interpret as signaling a major up or down move, depending on which way the wind is blowing at the time.

penny stocks Pipe dreams for sale.

pension fund What management just raided to finance a new corporate jet.

perpetual bond A bond that offers hope of recovering the principal.

pig An investor who tries to squeeze the last few points of a price swing and gets slaughtered.

pink sheets A list of risky ventures investors lose sleep over.

point and figure charting A form of technical analysis that can be hazardous to your financial health.

poison pill The ultimate defense for the crown jewels.

portfolio A dignified name for the collection of cats and dogs in which you've invested your life savings.

preemptive right A way for brokers to make two sales with one phone call.

preferred stock A class of stock more desirable in name only.

premium What you always pay, but never receive.

present value An economic analyst's term often used to deflate wishful thinking.

price-earnings (P/E) ratio A measure of value often used to convince you to continue holding a stock that has dropped through the floor.

price inertia Physics terminology that explains why your stocks aren't following the rally.

primary distribution The only sure way to make a million in the stock market.

prime rate To quote a major New York bank, "The prime rate is defined to be the rate of interest publicly announced by the bank as its prime rate."

principal Often confused with principle, a scarce commodity on Wall Street.

private placement A ground floor opportunity that might flood over before you can get your money out.

profit and loss statement Often, a more apt definition would delete the words "profit and."

profit margin A misnomer for the size of the loss expressed in percentage terms.

profit taking A term Wall Street columnists use to explain a downturn after a run-up in stocks you don't own.

program trading Computerized buying or selling of large numbers of stocks by institutions which can turn fads into trends and trends into disasters.

pro forma statement A rosy forecast used for raising money.

prospectus A flier on some speculative mining shares.

proxy Permission for the fox to manage the chicken coop.

prudent man rule What the trustees of your family's battered trust can prove they followed.

public offering An old Roman sacrificial custom adapted to the stock market.

put option What the smart money is buying on the stock you've just bought.

pyramiding Setting yourself up for King Tut's revenge.

qualified opinion The auditor's tactful suggestion that the client firm's accountants are incompetent, crooked, or both.

qualitative factors Reasons stocks often perform contrary to the expectations of security analysts.

quality of earnings What your broker talks about when the quantity of earnings is low.

quarterly statement What investors use to find out how far off security analysts were on their earnings forecasts.

quick assets The first assets to disappear from a company with crooked management.

quotation The price at which you can never execute your order.

R

raider That social, moral, and financial degenerate whose only redeeming quality is a willingness to pay a lot more for your stock than it's worth now.

rally What your stocks and bonds need to do just to get you back to the breakeven point.

random walk hypothesis A simple explanation, which your broker never mentions, for why Forbes' Dart Fund often outperforms the Dow Jones Industrials.

ratio analysis Dividing a disheartening number by a discouraging number and getting a rosy result.

real estate An investment that shows a paper loss on April 15 and a cash profit on April 16.

Real Estate Investment Trust (REIT) A real estate investment offering a high yield on questionable assets.

real rate of interest An attempt by economists to persuade everyone that interest rates aren't as high as they seem.

recapitalization A way to get run over by the same truck twice.

receivership A football term applied to finance that, loosely interpreted, means the opposition intercepted and ran it back for the winning touchdown.

redemption The religious concept of hope applied to the bond market.

redeployment of assets What financial managers do when their Far Eastern competition cuts prices.

red herring The one shining example of truth in advertising in the securities industry.

refunding What reputable department stores do that brokers don't.

Reg A A song and dance act used to promote small issues of securities.

registered representative A fancy title for a telephone sales jockey.

registration A detailed statement of financial data made prior to a public offering, understandable only to accountants and lawyers.

Regulation T A margin requirement enforced by Mr. T.

reinvestment rate What you will earn on your bond coupons, assuming you receive them.

reorganization A dignified name for bankruptcy.

repatriation of profits What your company would do with its foreign profits, if it had any.

replacement cost An optimistic method for evaluating a company's assets.

repurchase agreement (REPO) A security so bad that, to sell it, you have to agree to buy it back.

reserves What bankrupt banks and brokerage firms don't have when they need them most.

resistance level What's supposed to prevent a stock you just sold from rallying to new highs.

restructuring A euphemism for "Well, it didn't work that way, so how about this?"

retained earnings The dividends you don't receive.

return on assets What you're more likely to get from the rear end of a small donkey.

return on equity What goes down when management's salaries go up.

return on investment As Will Rogers once said, "What you should really be concerned with is the return *of* your investment."

revenue bonds A bad way to finance a hamburger stand.

reverse split The only way some stocks' prices will ever rise.

rights Investment options which, if not exercised, turn into wrongs.

risk A factor shared by speculators trying to double their money overnight and savers who hide their money in their mattresses.

risk averse A quality that bankers share with ostriches.

rollover What your dog can do better than your bond broker.

round lot What the big boys buy.

run up What usually happens right after you short a stock.

S

safe harbor What boats can find, but money can't.

sale and leaseback A way to sell your cake and eat it too.

scalper A market maker who learned his trade at Little Big Horn.

scrip What in the future will be called scrap.

seasonal fluctuation Your broker's euphemism for a 100-point drop in the Dow.

seasonal issues Stocks which enjoy a brief moment of glory each year — like pigs in April, turkeys in November, and geese in December.

seat An informal name for membership in the most expensive club in the world.

secondary distribution A second chance for the principals to bail out before the ship goes down.

secured loan What all the other lenders had.

Securities and Exchange Commission (SEC) A federal agency that protects investors by raising the cost of doing business on Wall Street.

security analyst A highly trained professional whose job it is to recommend stocks at the precise moment that they reach their yearly highs.

selling climax A moment of intense pleasure experienced by short sellers when the bottom drops out of the market.

serial bonds Bonds worth less than two Wheaties' box tops.

short sale Selling securities you don't own: a crime anywhere but on Wall Street.

short term To vulgarize Professor Keynes, a period of time when we all wish we were dead.

sinking fund Money set aside to plug leaks or buy bigger bailing pumps.

sleeper A stock whose value is recognized by the market after you sell it.

Sleeping Beauty A potential takeover target that has not yet been kissed by Prince Charming.

small cap stocks A more appropriate name would be "hard hat stocks" — securities suitable only for investors wearing crash helmets.

smart money The fat cats who buy what you're selling and sell what you're buying.

soft dollars What money managers use to reimburse brokerage firms for essential services, such as greens fees at exclusive golf clubs and deep-sea fishing trips.

soft market Where you take hard knocks.

south Where you plan to take a winter vacation — if your stocks don't go there first.

specialist An official responsible for maintaining a fair and orderly market for a security, unless it's profitable to do otherwise.

special situation An investment whose most special feature is how long you have to hold it before it moves.

speculation An investment before it goes belly up.

spinoff A subsidiary originally purchased at a premium, now sold off at a discount.

split How management keeps a stock attractive to small investors after a large advance so the large investors can bail out.

spot market Where you're taken to the cleaners while you're still wearing your clothes.

spread A futures trading technique that's like riding two horses at a time in opposite directions.

stabilization The quiet that comes after a 100-point drop in the Dow.

Standard & Poor's 500 Stocks that are long on pedigree and short on performance.

statistics Impressive documentation for bald-faced lies.

stockbroker 1. What a kid from a wealthy family becomes when he graduates from college and still doesn't know what he wants to be when he grows up. **2.** A financial salesman whose credibility ranks just below that of a used car salesman. **3.** Someone who, as Woody Allen once said, "invests your money until it's all gone." **4.** What many waiters were before switching to a more lucrative career.

stock dividend Less appealing than cash, but better than nothing.

stop order What you should have put in two weeks ago.

straddle An extremely awkward position which results from either buying or selling both a put and a call with equally bad striking prices.

strap What you find yourself in when you own both a straddle and a call.

street name A way to own securities under an alias.

striking price A military term which conveys the damage that can result from the price at which your options transaction is executed.

subordinated bonds Formal acknowledgment that the other bonds are better than yours.

sunk cost As your broker explains, "In for a dime, in for a dollar."

supply-side economics What you pin your hopes on when demand-side economics doesn't work.

support level What's supposed to prevent a stock you've just bought from breaking down to new lows.

switching A railroad term for being thrown off the main line.

syndicate A sinister but appropriate name for a group of investment bankers.

takeover bid Good news for shareholders and brokers; bad news for management.

taking a flier Speculating on a stock that could crash at any moment.

tax deduction A legal way to reduce your taxes, as long as the IRS doesn't inspect your documentation.

tax-exempt bonds Bonds whose yield is so low that the government doesn't have the heart to tax them.

tax reform Legislation that benefits politicians, lawyers, and accountants.

tax refund Like Santa Claus and the tooth fairy: a myth.

tax shelter A straw house that the IRS tries to blow down.

technical analysis The Wall Street equivalent of astrology.

technical downturn A drop in prices that no one can explain.

technical rally A rise in prices that no one can explain.

tender offer A term of endearment used to seduce shareholders into surrendering their stock in an acquisition.

theoretical value A value no one believes.

thin stock A stock that's hard to buy and harder to sell.

third market The financial equivalent of a lesser-developed country.

thrift institution A lending company that pays less than the current market rate of return on your deposits while simultaneously refusing your home loan application.

ticker A news service that often proves the maxim that no news is good news.

tight money An economic condition that exists when your friendly banker asks *you* for a loan.

time value The premium that investors put on time, which explains why investors are lousy lovers.

timing A surefire method to make money, just as the rhythm method is a surefire way to avoid pregnancy.

tip Advice that is either worthless, illegal, or both.

tombstone ad A burial announcement for your hot new issue that arrived D.O.A.

trader An investment professional whose loyalty is as much in question as his advice.

trading post A term that brings to mind the Wild West, where Indians exchanged buffalo hides for worthless trinkets.

transaction costs What often dwarfs trading profits on active accounts.

transfer tax How the New York state taxing authorities profit every time you buy or sell.

Treasury bills (T bills) Securities every bit as safe as the U.S. Government.

Treasury stock Stock the company had to buy because no one else wanted it.

trend analysis A method of predicting the future that can be used by anyone who can draw a straight line with a ruler.

trickle down An economic theory that asserts that the best way to promote growth is to let the rich get richer so their wealth can "trickle down" to the less fortunate, e.g. in the form of tips to washroom attendants.

trustee Someone who holds title to or administers assets for another; not to be confused with "trusty."

turkeys What most special situations turn out to be.

turnover What your stomach does while you're watching the ticker tape.

U

uncertainty One thing you can always count on in the market.

undercapitalized The financial condition of a business whose accounts payable department is a lot busier than its accounts receivable department.

undervalued securities Your portfolio.

underwriter An investment banker who distributes new issues that are sure winners to his best customers, and new issues that aren't to you.

unissued stock Shares so risky that underwriters are afraid to sell them.

unlisted security Unlike an unlisted phone number, a security you can find but may wish you hadn't.

unseasoned issues Stocks that the Food and Drug Administration has not approved.

unsecured bond A bond that may or may not be worth the paper it's printed on.

uptick What usually happens right after you sell a stock.

variable annuity A way to get savaged by a life insurance company before you die.

volatility A measure of how any investment vehicle compares with a roller coaster.

volume What analysts talk about when there's nothing more exciting going on.

voting rights What shareholders have in common with citizens of the Soviet Union.

wallflower A stock that can't get a date.

Wall Street 1. Where everyone tries to use inside information for personal profit, and those who succeed are jailed. **2.** Where sky diving records are registered during market crashes. **3.** The first place in America to legalize gambling.

"Wall Street Week" A TV show run by a man who looks like George Washington and sounds like Henny Youngman.

warrant What the sheriff should obtain for the arrest of any friend who gives you a hot tip.

wash sale A broker's way of wringing a commission out of you at year end to pay his holiday bills.

when issued A confusing term that indicates a security may be issued if anyone wants to buy it.

white knight A chivalrous investor who rescues management but leaves the stockholders stranded.

widow-and-orphan stock A stock that pays high dividends and is very safe . . . until its monopoly position is threatened by anti-trust enforcement.

windows Glass openings in Wall Street office buildings that let in light and let out despondent investors.

working capital What your capital refuses to be.

World Bank A charitable institution that lends only to countries that can't possibly repay their loans.

WPPSS bonds Proof that bond ratings are not infallible.

Yankee bonds Imagine letting George Steinbrenner and Billy Martin manage your investments — together.

yield What goes up, along with your blood pressure, when the stock price goes down.

yield curve A graph that shows how much your bonds give up over time.

yield rally A Wall Street euphemism for a sharp decline in bond prices.

yield to broker A sign posted in many Wall Street restrooms to enable brokers to get back to their telephones ASAP.

yield to maturity What you earn on your bonds if the company survives.

yo-yo stock A volatile stock suitable only for the young at heart.

Z

zero-based budgeting A way to manage spending by justifying all expenditures except the bonuses for top management.

zero coupon bond A corporate bond that pays no interest and offers a "guaranteed return" only if it happens to mature.

Mother Murphy's Law
by Bruce Lansky

The wit of Bombeck and the wisdom of Murphy are combined in this collection of 32 laws that detail the perils and pitfalls of parenthood. Cartoon illustrations by Christine Tripp. **$2.95**

Ordering #: 1149

Mother Murphy's 2nd Law
by Bruce Lansky

A ribald collection of laws about love, sex, marriage and other skirmishes in the battle the sexes. Mother Murphy offers rib-tickling advice to singles, marrieds and the divorced that they won't find in marriage and sex manuals. **$2.95**

Ordering #: 4010

Grandma Knows Best
by Mary McBride

Mary McBride instructs grandmas who have been stuck with babysitting how to "scheme, lie, cheat, and threaten so you'll be thought as a sweet, darling grandma." **$4.95**

Ordering #: 4009

Webster's Dictionary Game
by Wilbur Webster

Dictionary Game fans will love this wacky word game invented by the black sheep of the famous dictionary family. Includes a special dictionary of over 5,000 esoteric words.
$5.95

Ordering #: 6030

ORDER FORM

Qty.	Book Title	Author	Price
____	Asian Customs and Manners	Chambers, K.	$ 7.95
____	Best Baby Shower Book, The	Cooke, C.	$ 4.95
____	Best European Travel Tips	Whitman, J.	$ 6.95
____	Best Wedding Shower Book, The	Cooke, C.	$ 4.95
____	David, We're Pregnant!	Johnston, L.	$ 3.95
____	Don't Call Mommy at Work Today Unless the Sitter Runs Away	McBride, M.	$ 4.95
____	Do They Ever Grow Up?	Johnston, L.	$ 3.95
____	European Customs and Manners	Braganti/Devine	$ 6.95
____	Grandma Knows Best	McBride, M.	$ 4.95
____	Hi Mom! Hi Dad!	Johnston, L.	$ 3.95
____	How to Find Romance in the Personals	Price/Dana	$ 4.95
____	How to Survive High School, with minimal brain damage	Lansky/Dorfman	$ 4.95
____	Letters From a Pregnant Coward	Armor, J.	$ 6.95
____	Lexicon of Intentionally Ambiguous Recommendations (LIAR)	Thornton, R.	$ 4.95
____	Mother Murphy's Law	Lansky, B.	$ 2.95
____	Mother Murphy's 2nd Law	Lansky, B.	$ 2.95
____	Successful Single Parenting	Wayman, A.	$ 4.95
____	Wall Street Bull	Lansky, B.	$ 4.95
____	Webster's Dictionary Game	Webster, W.	$ 5.95

Please send me copies of the books checked above. I am enclosing $ _____ which covers the full amount per book shown above plus $1.25 for postage and handling for the first book and $.50 for each additional book. (Add $2.00 to total for postage and handling for books shipped to Canada. Overseas postage and handling will be billed. MN residents add 6% sales tax.) Allow up to four weeks for delivery. **Quantity discounts available upon request.**

Send check or money order to Meadowbrook, Inc. No cash or C.O.D.s, please.

For purchases over $10.00, you may use VISA or MasterCard (order by mail or phone). For these orders we need information below.
Charge to: ☐ **VISA**   ☐ **MasterCard**

Account # _____

Expiration Date _____

Card Signature _____

Send Book(s) to:

Name _____

Address _____

City _____ State _____ Zip _____
Mail order to: Book Orders, Meadowbrook, Inc., 18318 Minnetonka Blvd., Deephaven, MN 55391. Phone orders: Toll Free (800) 338-2232.